Libellus de Historia

Latin History Reader
for use with

Latin for Children: Primer A

Acknowledgements

Classical Academic Press would like to thank **Gaylan Dubose** for his expertise and care in editing this text.

Libellus de Historia

Latin History Reader for use with
Latin for Children: Primer A

Classical Academic Press, 2005
Version 4

Classical Academic Press
3920 Market Street
Camp Hill, PA 17011

www.ClassicalAcademicPress.com

ISBN: 9781600510045

Book design & cover by:
Rob Baddorf

"Cui dono lepidum novum libellum . . ."
-Catullus

With thanks to my mother, Pam Tobola, who *made* me study Latin. You set me on a grand adventure to the ancient world of Rome which has never ceased to fascinate me.

Latin For Children, Primer A
HISTORY READER

Contents

Contents

Libellus dē Historiā, Pars A

A Little Book about History, Part A

Latin, the language of the great Roman Empire; an Empire which at one time ruled nearly the entire civilized world, which saw the downfall of many great kingdoms and empires, which witnessed the rise of a different kingdom known as Christendom. Libellus dē Historiā invites you to explore the history witnessed by the Romans through their own native tongue. From Augustus to Constantine, from the birth of Christ to the Nicene Creed, these 15 short stories track the progress of the Roman Empire and the rise of Christianity. Latin students will discover some of history's most exciting events while applying the grammar tools of Latin that they have acquired.

Each story is keyed to the Latin grammar and vocabulary taught in Latin for Children, Primer A and the history taught through the Veritas Press New Testament, Greece & Rome History Series. While the reader was originally conceived as a supplemental text to enhance the learning experience of the student using these curricula, it is not necessary to use either of them to benefit from and enjoy this reader. This little book has a user-friendly format in order to provide full support for even the most novice Latin teachers, regardless of the curriculum they choose.

This first reader in the Libellus dē Historiā series assumes that students have not had any previous translation experience. The reader, therefore, introduces students to story translation. Each story is written not as a formal paragraph, but as a series of numbered sentences. Each sentence builds on those preceding it in order to tell a story. Thus, students are not overwhelmed by the size of the story in its entirety, but are able to focus on one sentence at a time.

Several helpful features are included to make this text easy to use by students, teachers, and parents. One feature is a Table of

Contents listing the grammar assumed for each story. This enables teachers to better select the appropriate material for their young translators. In addition, each story glosses all new vocabulary words not already taught in previous chapters of LFC's Primer A, or seen in previous stories. A full Glossary is also included, listing every word used throughout the reader. Each entry is accompanied by a reference to the chapter in which that word first appears. In this edition we have also included many grammatical and historical notes alongside the vocabulary words for each chapter. These notes will provide readers with further insight into the etymology or meaning of some words, and the history associated with others.

Finally, I would like to share with you my approach for both written and oral translations. This process is one I developed in my own classroom through the years; I find it to be very beneficial. Whether you choose this approach or develop one of your own, maintaining a consistent and systematic method of translating will make the experience more enjoyable for both students and teachers.

Step 1: Unfamiliar Vocabulary List

Students should make a list of all vocabulary they do not recognize or whose meaning they are uncertain of. While all vocabulary not glossed with a particular story is assumed to have already been learned or seen in previous chapters, students may have yet to seal these words in their minds. Putting this step before the actual translation may seem tedious at first. However, I guarantee that this discipline will make the translation process much smoother. Moreover, this exercise will reinforce the students' developing vocabulary and memorization skills. The more often a student must look up a given word, whose meaning eludes him, the better he will learn that word.

Step 2: Written Translation:

I generally advise that students be divided into groups of two to three for this task. Particularly in the beginning, students will find some security and confidence in working together. However, I find that groups larger than three have a more difficult time collaborating effectively to obtain a good translation. Other times, you may wish to have students work independently.

Latin sentence structure is more loose than English, but most prose does follow certain rules. Thus, each sentence may be approached with a Question and Answer Flow which should be familiar to students of Shurley Grammar. For the sentences in this reader, this simple question pattern should suffice:

1. Where is the Verb (Linking or Action)? Parse: Tense, Person, Number
2. Where is the Subject? Parse: Case, Number, Gender
3. Any Adjectives modifying the Subject? Parse: Case, Number, Gender.
4. Do we need a Direct Object or Predicate? Why? Parse: Case, Number, Gender
5. Any Adjectives modifying the D.O. /P.N.? Parse: Case, Number, Gender.
6. Are there any Prepositions? What case does the Preposition take? Where is the Object of the Preposition? Parse: Case, Number, Gender
7. Any Adjectives modifying the O.P.? Parse: Case, Number, Gender.
8. Any word(s) left? Parse: Case, Number, Gender or Tense, Person, Number
    How does this word fit in our sentence? Why?

Repeat this process for each sentence and each subordinate clause within a sentence.

Step 3: Oral Translation

Many classrooms may wish to end the translation process with a written exercise. While that is certainly a sufficient end for some, I feel they are missing out on a wonderful opportunity. Oral translation is my favorite part of Latin class both as a student and as a teacher. This is a wonderful exercise that has so many benefits. First, it builds great confidence in the students for they are truly reading a Latin story. Second, it works to develop oral language skills, which students will need in learning any modern language they may choose to study. Finally, oral practice helps in laying a foundation for the Rhetoric Stage, the capstone of the Trivium.

If possible, arrange students in a circle or other arrangement that enables class members to participate and interact well with one another and the teacher. Allow them their Latin passage and unfamiliar vocabulary list, but do not allow them their English translations. We all know that they can read English; this exercise is to practice reading Latin.

Before you begin reading, it is important to give everyone, including the teacher, permission to make mistakes, no matter how big they seem. No one is fluent in Latin yet. We are all learning.

One by one have students read aloud; first in Latin then in English. If a student appears to be stuck guide them through the sentence using the questions listed above. Then, ask them to re-translate the sentence smoothly on their own. Occasionally ask a student to re-translate a sentence already translated by someone else, but in a slightly different way.

Step 4: Reading Comprehension

Teaching students how to read for comprehension and specific information is an important goal at the grammar stage. It need not be limited to English grammar classes. Each story in this reader is followed by a few reading comprehension questions. They may certainly be used as a written exercise. However, I recommend asking them orally following the time of oral translation. It gives students a thrill to know they are having a Latin conversation, while at the same time exercising both their oral and reading comprehension skills.

As you read through these stories, be sure to take the time not only to enjoy the vocabulary and grammar contained in this little book, but the stories used to demonstrate them as well. Each one of the fifteen stories was written with a desire to enhance the young translator's understanding of the people and culture of ancient Rome. Learn what secret weapon Hannibal used to defeat the Romans, who fought at the Battle of Actium, and why the Flavian Amphitheatre became known as the Colosseum. Each of these events occurred while Rome ruled the Mediterranean and each was recorded for posterity by the great historians of the day in Latin, Rome's mother tongue. Students are sure to enjoy deciphering their own Latin records of Rome's history in Libellus dē Historiā.

CAPUT I

Vitruvius et Architectūra

1. Vitruvius Pollio est Rōmānus Architectus.

2. Amat architectūram Graecam.

3. Aedificat multa aedificia.

4. Vitruvius scrībit, "Decem Librī dē Architectūrā."

Vitruvius et Architectūra

GLOSSARY:

<u>Vitruvius Pollio,</u> nominative, m., sing., Vitruvius Pollio (name)

<u>architectūra, ae,</u> f., architecture

<u>Graecus, a, um,</u> adj., Greek

> architectūram Graecam, The Romans adopted much of their architectural style from the Greeks.

<u>scrībō, scrībere,</u> to write

> scrībit, present tense of scrībere. This is a verb of the 3rd conjugation, which will be taught in LFC, Primer B. The personal endings of the 3rd conjugation are identical to those of the 1st & 2nd conjugations in the present tense.

<u>multus, a, um,</u> adj. many

<u>aedificō, aedificāre,</u> to build

<u>decem,</u> indeclinable adj., ten

<u>liber, librī,</u> m., book

<u>dē,</u> prep. + ablative = about

<u>Decem Librī dē Architectūrā,</u> Vitruvius's work consists of 10 volumes discussing the architecture of various types of buildings during the late Republic and early Empire. Several are dedicated to the well known amphitheatres. This work was widely read and referred to by architects of the Renaissance period. Vitruvius is believed to have been held in favor by Julius Caesar during his years of prominence, and to have dedicated "dē Architectūrā" to the Emperor Augustus.

RESPONDĒ LATĪNE :

1.   Quis est Vitruvius?

2.   Quid aedificat?

Quis – who?   Quid – what?

CAPUT II

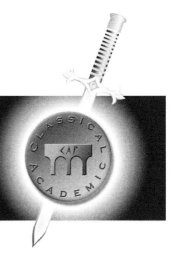

Hannibal

1. Hannibal est Pūnicus dux.

2. Habet multās cōpiās et multōs elephantōs.

3. Virī exercent elephantōs pugnāre.

4. Hannibal et Pūnicae cōpiae et elephantī oppugnābunt

Rōmānōs.

5. Est Secundum Pūnicum Bellum.

GLOSSARY:

<u>Hannibal</u>, nominative, m., sing., Hannibal

<u>dux</u>, nominative, m., sing., leader

<u>Pūnicus, a, um</u>, adj., Carthaginian, Punic

> From this adjective, meaning Carthaginian, it becomes clear why the Roman wars against the Carthaginians are referred to as the Punic Wars.

<u>cōpiae, ārum</u>, f. pl., troops

> This noun may have been taught as 'supply, abundance' (cf. corn of copia). However, in the plural form it is often used as a military term meaning 'troops'.

<u>elephantus, ī</u>, m., elephant

<u>secundus, a, um</u>, adj., second

<u>est</u>, When beginning a sentence, this linking verb may use the pronouns 'this' or 'there' as a subject instead of the more commonly seen 'he/she/it'.

<u>bellum, ī</u>, n., war

RESPONDĒ LATĪNĒ :

1. Quis est Hannibal?

2. Quid Pūnicī virī exercent?

Quis – who? Quid – what?

CAPUT III

Iulius Caesar

1. Populī amant Iulium Caesarem.

2. Senātorēs nōn amant Iulium.

3. Iulius approprinquat.

4. Eheu! Inīmicī necant Iulium!

5. Populī sunt īrātī! Inimicī currunt!

GLOSSARY:

<u>Iulius Caesar</u> – nominative, masculine, sing. – Julius Caesar

<u>populus</u> – This singular noun refers to a large people group such as a nation or tribe. It is, however, still a singular noun and must be accompanied by a singular verb.

<u>Caesarem</u>, accusative, m., sing., Caesar

<u>Senātorēs</u>, nominative, m., pl., Senators

> Both Caesar and Senator are nouns of the 3rd declension (taught in LFC, Primer B), so their endings are unfamiliar. These words have both been adopted into our own English language without any spelling changes.

<u>appropinquō, appropinquāre</u>, to approach

<u>eheu</u>, exclamation, Alas!

<u>inimīcī</u>, Remember, this word is used for a personal enemy. Some of the senators were personal enemies of Caesar, but not necessarily enemies of the Roman people. A foreign enemy attacking the state would be referred to as hostis, from which we derive "hostile".

<u>currō, currere</u>, to run

RESPONDĒ LATĪNĒ:

1. Quī amant Caesarem?

2. Quī sunt inimīcī ?

Quī - who? (plural)

CAPUT IV

Octavius

1. Octavius et Antonius simul regēbānt Imperium Rōmānum.

2. Octavius manēbat in Italiā.

3. Antonius et Cleopātra erant in Aegyptō.

4. Octavius oppugnat Antonium et Cleopātram.

5. Ocatvius est victor!

6. Nunc, sōlus Octavius regit Imperium Rōmānum.

GLOSSARY:

Octavius, Octaviī, m., Octavian

Antonius, ī, m., Antony

simul, adv., together

regō, regere, to rule

> This verb belongs to the 3rd conjugation which will be taught in LFC, Primer B. This conjugation is identified by a short 'e' in the infinitive (cf. regere vs. manēre). The personal endings for the present and imperfect tenses are the same as those for the 1st and 2nd conjugation.

imperium, imperiī, n., empire

Rōmānus, a, um, adj., Roman

in, prep. + ablative = in, on

Cleopātra, ae, f., Cleopatra

victor, nominative, m., sing., victor

nunc, adv., now

sōlus, a, um, adj., only, alone

Nota Bene:

This story refers to the Battle of Actium which was fought in 31 B.C. Octavian's decisive victory over Antony and Cleopatra solidified his sole rule over the entire Roman Empire. Many historians consider the reign of Augustus to have begun with this great victory. The Senate, however, did not bestow the title of "Augustus" on Octavian until a few years later.

RESPONDĒ LATĪNĒ:

1.   Ubī erat Octavius?

2.   Ubī erant Antonius et Cleopātra?

Ubī – where?

CAPUT V

Partus Christī

1. Iosephus ambulābat Bethlemam. Asinus portābat Mariam.

2. Iosephus erat sordidus. Maria erat dēfessa. Asinus erat odōrātus.

3. Dēnique, veniunt Bethlemam, sed cauponae sunt plēnae.

4. Iosephus, Maria, et asinus manent in stabulō.

5. Iesus nascitur in stabulō. Multī mīrī angelī cantant, "Glōria! Glōria!"

GLOSSARY:

<u>partus</u>, nominative, m., sing., birth

> Partus is actually a noun of the 4th declension. Its nominative singular appears the same as that of the 2nd declension masculine.

<u>Iosephus</u>, ī, m., Joseph

<u>Bethlema</u>, ae, f., Bethlehem

> <u>ambulābat Bethlemam</u> = he was walking to Bethlehem

> The names of towns do not use a Latin preposition to show motion toward or away from that place.

<u>asinus</u>, ī, m., donkey

<u>Maria</u>, ae, f., Mary

<u>odōrātus</u>, a, um, adj., smelly

<u>dēnique</u>, adv., finally

<u>veniō, venire</u>, to come

> This is a 4th conjugation verb (taught in LFC, primer C). 4th conjugation verbs use the same personal endings as verbs of the first two conjugations.

<u>caupona</u>, ae, f., inn

<u>in</u>, prep.+ ablative, in, on

> This preposition has a different meaning when it is used with the accusative case as in chapter 4. (This difference will be explained in chapters 25 and 29 of LFC, Primer A.)

<u>stabulum</u>, ī, n., stable

<u>nascitur</u> = he is born

<u>angelus</u>, ī, m., angel

Partus Christī

RESPONDĒ LATĪNĒ:

1. Quis est dēfessa?

2. Quis est odōrātus?

3. Ubī Iosephus et Maria manent? Cūr?

Quis – who? Ubī – where? Cūr – why?

CAPUT VI

Mīrus Vir

1. Iohannes est mīrus vir.

2. Gestat capillum camēlī. Edit ferum favum et lōcustās.

3. Monet Iudaeōs "Parāte! Fīlius Deī venit!"

4. "Baptizō aquā, sed baptizābit flammīs."

GLOSSARY

hannes, nominative, m., sing., John

stō, gestāre, to wear

mēlus, ī, m., camel

ō, edere, to eat

rus, a, um, adj., wild (cf. ferus, ī, m. wild animal; Ch. 9 of LFC, primer
)

vus, ī, m., honeycomb

custa, ae, f., locust

daeī , ōrum, m., Jews

eī, genitive, m., sing. = of God

> The genitive case often shows possession.

ptizō, āre, to baptize

> This Latin word is derived from the Greek βαπτιζώ, which means
> submerge in water.

d, conj., but

mma, ae, f., flame, fire

> flammīs, aquā, ablative. Remember the Ablative Case can use the
> prepositions "by, with, from." Which one works best here?

ESPONDĒ LATĪNĒ:

Quis est mīrus vir?

Quid Iohannes edit?

Quis baptizābit flammīs?

ıis – who? Quid – what?

CAPUT VII

Iesus

1. Iesus ambulat ad multa oppida.

2. Sedet apud populōs, et nārrat multās parabolās.

3. Parabolae dēmōnstrant regnum Deī.

4. Iesus amat populōs et multī populī amant Iesum.

5. Sed aliī populī erunt contrā Iesum.

GLOSSARY:

sedeō, sedēre, to sit

parabola, ae, f., parable

> This Latin word is derived from the Greek παραβολή, meaning a parable or proverb.

regnum, ī, n., kingdom

Deī, genitive, m., sing., of God

alius, alia, aliud, adj., other

RESPONDĒ LATĪNĒ:

1. Quandō Iesus ambulat?

2. Quid Iesus nārrat?

3. Quōs Iesus amat?

Quandō – to where? Quid – what?
Quōs (acc. , pl.) – whom?

CAPUT VIII

Iesus est Vīvus!

1. Rōmānī necant Iesum, quod Iūdaeī ducēs timent Iesum.

2. Signum est suprā Iesum. Nārrat, "Rēx Iudaeōrum."

3. Post trēs diēs, Iesus resurgit.

4. Multī populī vident Iesum et ambulant cum Iesō.

5. Iesus est vīvus; Iesus erit vīvus semper!

Iesus est Vīvus!

GLOSSARY:

cāre, This word may be translated as to kill or to execute.

od, conj., because

daeus, a, um, adj., Jewish

neō, timēre, to fear, be afraid of

cēs, nominative, m., pl., leaders

x, nominative, m., sing., king

> Rēx Iudaeōrum – As was the Roman custom, a sign was placed on the cross above those crucified naming the charge against them. In the case of Jesus' execution, the charge was that he claimed to be, "King of the Jews." This charge was written on the sign in three languages: Latin, Greek, and Aramaic. Today, many replicas of the crucificixion will place a small sign with "R.I." (Rex Iudaeōrum) inscribed upon it.

s diēs, accusative, pl., three days

urgō, resurgere, to rise again

us, a, um, adj., alive

nper, adv., always

ESPONDĒ LATĪNĒ:

Quī timent Iesum?

Quid signum nārrat?

Estne Iesus vīvus?

ī (plural) – who? Quid – what? Estne – is?
nime – no! Ita vero – yes!

CAPUT IX

Nero

1. Post Rōma flagrat, Nero aedificat multa suprā ruīnās.

2. Nero aedificat magnam Domum Auream intrā Rōmam.

3. Aedificat Colossum, magnam statuam nūdī Nerōnis, prope Domum Auream.

4. Post multōs annōs, Titus Flavius Vespasiānus aedificat magnum amphitheātrum iuxtā Colossum.

5. Rōmānī appellant Flaviānum Amphitheātrum "Colossēum" quod est iuxtā Colossum Nerōnis.

GLOSSARY:

post, adv., This word has been taught as a preposition taking the accusative case. It may also act alone as an adverb, as it does in the first sentence.

flagrō, flagrāre, to burn

Nero, nominative, m., sing., Nero

> Nerōnis, genitive = of Nero

multa, neuter pl. = many things

> This is a substantive adjective, meaning that it is standing alone without a noun. The word "things" is often understood in translating these adjectives when they are neuter.

ruina, ae, f., ruin, debris

Domum Auream, accusative, f., sing., Golden House

> Although domus may appear to be a masculine second declension noun, it is a fourth declension feminine noun. Therefore both magnam and auream are correctly placed in the feminine gender.

Colossus, ī, m., Colossus

amphitheātrum, ī, n., amphitheatre

Titus Flavius Vespasianus – The full name of both emperors Vespasian and his son Titus. The building of the Colosseum was begun by Vespasian. However he died when only the first two stories had been built. Construction was completed during the reign of his son, Titus. It was initially called the Flavian Amphitheatre, having been built during the Flavian Dynasty. However, it later came to be called the Colosseum due to its location next to the Colossus of Nero, no longer standing.

Flavianus, a, um, adj., Flavian (built by Flavius)

Colossēum, ī, n., Colosseum

RESPONDĒ LATĪNĒ:

1. Quid Nero aedificat?

2. Quid Vespasianus aedificat?

Quid – what?

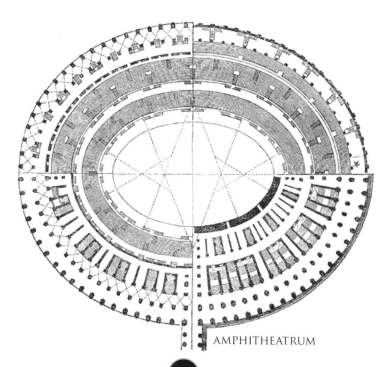

AMPHITHEATRUM

CAPUT X

Arcus Titī

1. Iūdaeī optant pugnāre contrā Rōmānōs.

2. Titus et Rōmānae copiae eunt Hierosolymōs.

3. Iūdaeī aedificant altum et longum mūrum circā oppidum.

4. Rōmānī eunt per mūrum. Dēlent templum.

5. Arcus Titī dēmōnstrat Titum et praemia Iūdaea.

GLOSSARY:

<u>Titus, ī</u>, m., Titus

<u>copiae, ārum</u>, f. pl., troops

<u>Hierosolyma, ōrum</u>, m. pl., Jerusalem

> This second declension masculine noun is plural in form, but singular in meaning.

<u>dēleō, dēlēre</u>, to destroy

<u>Arcus Titī</u> = The Arch of Titus

> The Arch of Titus stands near the Colosseum built by the Emperor Titus and his father, Vespasian. The triumphal arch shows pictures of the emperor carrying the treasures of the Jewish temple.

RESPONDĒ LATĪNĒ:

1. Quid Iūdaeī aedificant?

2. Quid Arcus dēmōnstrat?

Quid – what?

CAPUT XI

Vesuvius

1. Vesuvius est altus mons in Italiā.

2. Pompēiī et Herculāneum erant oppida prope Vesuvium.

3. Multī populī habitābant in oppidīs.

4. Multī Rōmānī ibant ad oppida per fēriās.

5. Subitō, Vesuvius ērumpit!

6. Nunc populī eunt ad oppida et vident ruīnās.

Vesuvius

GLOSSARY:

Vesuvius, ī, m., Vesuvius

mōns, nominative, m., sing., mountain

Italia, ae, f., Italy

Pompēiī , ōrum, m. pl., Pompeii

> Like Hierosolyma (Jerusalem) in the previous chapter, this noun is plural in form but singular in meaning.

Herculāneum, ī, n., Herculaneum

fēriae, ārum, f. pl., holidays, vacation

> This is another word that is always plural in form. Vacations usually last for more than one day. Holidays in ancient Rome could last for several days, even weeks!

subitō, adv., suddenly

ērumpō, ērumpere, to erupt, explode

ruīna, ae, f., ruin, debris

RESPONDĒ LATĪNĒ:

1. Ubī est Vesuvius?

2. Ubī erant Pompēiī et Herculāneum?

Ubī – where?

Pessimī Imperātōrēs

1. Diocletianus regit Rōmānum Imperium cum Maximianō.

2. Appellant sē Iovem et Herculum.

3. Vexant Christianōs sine clēmentiā.

4. Prohibent Christianōs congrēgāre.

5. Prehendunt Christianōs, nisi adorābunt falsōs deōs.

6. Cremant sanctōs librōs.

GLOSSARY:

imperātōrēs, nominative, m., pl., emperors

Diocletianus, ī, m., Diocletian

Maximianus, ī, m., Maximian

appellō, appellāre, to call, address

sē, pronoun, accusative, m., pl., themselves

Iovem, accusative, m., sing., Jove, Juppiter

Herculus, ī, m., Hercules (demi-god and son of Juppiter)

> Iovem et Herculum – Soon after coming into supreme power, Diocletian and Maximian began referring to themselves as Juppiter and Hercules. Such references have been found on the coins made with their likenesses. To the Romans such titles were interpreted as "Supreme Commander" and "Man of Action" respectively. Emperors often tried to associate their names with those of the gods although none were actually deified until after their death. It was, however, unusual for an emperor to actually assume the name of a god during his life. Perhaps their desire for their own divinity prompted their aggressive hatred of the monotheistic Christians.

vexō, vexāre, to annoy, harass

Christianus, ī, m., Christians, followers of Christ

clementia, ae, f., mercy

prohibeō, prohibēre, to forbid

nisi, conj., unless

cremō, cremāre, to burn to ashes

sanctus, a, um, adj., holy

Nota Bene:

While Diocletian and Maximian persecuted the Christians relentlessly, it may be interesting to note that Diocletian's own wife, Prisca, was a Christian. Maximian's son-in-law, Constantine the Great, would later become the first Christian Emperor, and undo the laws against Christians proclaimed by his father-in-law and predecessor.

RESPONDĒ LATĪNĒ:

1. Quī sunt pessimī imperātōrēs?

2. Quī sē appellant?

Quī (nom. pl.) – who?

CAPUT XIII

Constantinus

Constantinus pugnābat quod optābat esse Imperātor.

Subitō, in caelō videt crucem cum flammīs.

Audit, "in hōc signō, vincēs!"

Constantinus iubet copiās pōnere "XP" in scūtīs.

Iterum pugnant. Constantinus est victor!

Nunc Constantinus adōrat Christum.

Constantinus

GLOSSARY:

Constantinus, ī, m., Constantine

esse, **infinitive or second principal part of** *sum, esse* **- to be**

imperātor, nominative, m., sing., emperor

crucem, accusative, m., sing., cross

audiō, audīre, to hear

hōc signō = this sign

vincēs, future, 2nd person, sing. = you will conquer < vincō, vincere

> The future tense of the third and fourth conjugation is formed differently than verbs of the first and second. You will learn more about these conjugations in LFC Primers B and C.

pōnō, pōnere, to put, place

XP, The Greek letters *chi* and *rho*. They are the first two letters used in the spelling of Christ, **Χριστός**. These two letters have been commonly used throughout history as a symbol for Christ.

scūtum, ī, n., shield

iterum, adv., again

adōrō, adōrāre, to worship

RESPONDĒ LATĪNE:

1. Quid Constantinus videt?

2. Quid Constantinus audit?

3. Ubī copiae pōnunt signum?

Quid – what? Ubī – where?

CAPUT XIV

Credo

The following are excerpts taken from the Latin translation of the Nicene Creed. The words in [ ] have been added for clarity, and do not appear in the text of the creed.

1. Crēdō in ūnum Deum, Patrem omnipotentem, . . .

2. et [crēdō] in ūnum Dominum Iesum Christum, Fīlium Deī unigenitum, . .

3. et [crēdō] in Spīritum Sanctum, Dominum et vīvificantem,

4. et [crēdō] in ūnam sanctam catholicam et apostolicam Ecclēsiam.

GLOSSARY

<u>crēdō, crēdere</u>, to believe in, put one's trust into

> Crēdō is sometimes used with in and the accusative of person, particularly in ecclesiastical Latin. This emphasizes the idea of placing one's hope and trust 'into' the being of an omnipotent God.

<u>ūnus, a, um</u>, adj., one

<u>Patrem omnipotentem</u>, accusative, m., sing., omnipotent (all powerful) Father

<u>unigenitus, a, um</u>, adj., only begotten

> This is adjective is a compound word from ūnus (one, only) + gignere (to beget, birth.)

<u>sanctus, a, um</u>, adj., holy

<u>vīvificantem</u>, adj. masculine, singular, accusative, lifegiver

> This adjective is a compound word from vīvus (alive, living) + facere (to make).

<u>catholicus, a, um</u>, adj., universal

> This is a Latin derivative from the Greek καθολικος, meaning "in general", and has come to mean "general," or "universal." It does not here refer specifically to the Catholic Church of Rome as opposed to Protestant or any other denomination of Christian believers.

<u>apostolicus, a, um</u>, adj., apostolic

<u>ecclēsia, ae</u>, f., church

RESPONDĒ LATĪNĒ:

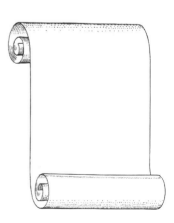

1. Quot sunt Deī?

2. Quis est Fīlius Deī?

Quot – how many? Quis – who?

CAPUT XV

Multī barbarī oppugnābant Rōmam.

Magnī ducēs aberant.

Multae familiae exeunt Rōmā.

Dēnique, barbarī ineunt Rōmam. Nunc regunt tōtam Italiam.

Rōmānum Imperium est nōn iam. Sed, tenēbimus Rōmam in memoriā semper.

Fīnis?

GLOSSARY:

<u>fīnis</u>, nominative, sing., end

<u>barbarus, ī</u>, m., barbarian, foreigner

<u>ducēs</u>, nominative, m., pl., leaders

<u>ineō, inīre</u>, to go into, enter

> exīre, inīre – note the contrast of the compound forms of the irregular verb ire (taught in ch. 30 of LFC, Primer A).

<u>Rōmā, Rōmam</u>, The names of towns in Latin do not require the addition of a Latin preposition to express motion "to" or "from." Instead the case normally required by that Latin preposition is used for the town's name.

> Rōmā in place of ē Rōmā
>
> Rōmam in place of ad Rōmam

<u>tōtus, a, um</u>, adj., all, whole, entire

<u>nōn iam</u>, adverbial phrase = no more

<u>tenēre in memoriā</u>, idiomatic expression, to remember

> This is an idiomatic expression commonly found in Latin prose and poetry. While literally translated as "to hold in memory," it may be more loosely translated as "to remember."

RESPONDĒ LATĪNĒ:

1. Quī exeunt Rōma?

2. Quī ineunt Rōmam?

3. Ubī est Rōma vīva?

Quī (nom. pl.) – who? Ubī = where?

Appendix A

Decem Rōmānī

(sing to the tune of "Ten Little Indians")

Ūnus, duo, trēs, Rōmānī

Quattuor, quinque, sex, Rōmānī

Septem, octo, novem, Rōmānī

Et decem Rōmānī.

Iesus Mē Amat

(sing to the tune of "Jesus Loves Me")

Iesus mē amat, hoc sciō.

Nam Biblia mī nārrant.

Līberī eī insunt; infirmī sunt, est fortis.

Iesus mē amat, Iesus mē amat,

Iesus mē amat, nam Biblia mī nārrant.

GLOSSARY:

<u>mē</u>, accusative, sing., me

<u>hoc</u>, accusative, sing., this

<u>nam</u>, adv., for

<u>Biblia</u>, n. pl., Bible

> This word is plural in form, but singular in meaning. The Bible is made up of many smaller books (i.e. Book of Proverbs, Book of Isaiah, Book of Matthew, etc.).

<u>mī</u>, dative, sing., to me (contracted form of mihi)

<u>eī</u>, dative, m., sing., to him

Latin For Children, Primer A
LATIN READER

Glossary

"Numbers in parentheses indicate the chapter in which the word first appears."

absum, abesse, āfuī, āfutūrum (15)	to be away, be absent
ad (5)	prep. + accusative, to, toward, at
adōrō, adōrāre, adōrāvī, adōrātum (13)	1, to worship, adore
aedificium, -ī (1)	n, building
aedificō, aedificāre, aedificāvī, aedificātum (1)	1, to build
Aegyptus, -ī (4)	m. Egypt
alius, -a, -um (7)	adj. other, another
altus, -a, -um (10)	adj. high
ambulō, ambulāre, ambulāvī, ambulātum (5)	1, to walk
amō, amāre, amāvī, amātum (1)	1, to love, like
amphitheātrum, -ī (9)	n. amphitheatre
angelus, -ī (5)	m. angel, messenger
annus, -ī (9)	m. year
Antoninus, -ī (4)	m. Antony
apostolicus, -a, -um (14)	adj. apostolic, pertaining to the original 12 apostles of Christ

Glossary

appellō, appellāre, appellāvī, appellātum (12)	1, to call, address
appropinquō, appropinquāre, appropinquāvī, appropinquātum (3)	1, to approach
apud (7)	prep. + accusative, with, near
aqua, -ae (6)	f. water
architectūra, -ae (1)	f. architecture
architectus, -ī (1)	m. architect
arcus, arcūs (10)	m. arch, triumphal arch
asinus, ī (5)	m. donkey
audiō, audīre, audīvī, audītum (13)	4, to hear, listen to
aureus, -a, -um (9)	adj. golden, of gold
baptizō, baptizāre, baptizāvī, baptizātum (6)	1, to baptise
barbarus, -ī (15)	m. barbarian, foreigner
bellum, -ī (2)	n, war
Bethlema, -ae (5)	f. Bethlehem
caelum, -ī (13)	n. sky
Caesar, Caesaris (3)	m. Caesar
camēlus, -ī (6)	m. camel
cantō, cantāre, cantāvī, cantātum (5)	1, to sing
capillus, -ī (6)	m. hair
catholicus, -a, um (14)	adj. universal, catholic
caupōna, -ae (5)	f. inn
Christiānus, -ī (12)	m. Christian
Christus, -ī (13)	m. Christ
circā (10)	prep. + accusative, around
clēmentia, -ae (12)	f. mercy

Glossary

Cleopātra, -ae (4)	f. Cleopatra
Colosseum, -ī (9)	n. Colosseum
colossus, -ī (9)	m. gigantic statue, colossus
Constantinus, -ī (13)	m. Constantine
contrā (7)	prep. + accusative, against
cōpia, -ae (2)	f. supply, abundance; (mil.) troops
crēdō, crēdere, crēdidī, creditum (14)	3, to believe, trust in (used with in + accusative of person)
cremō, cremāre, cremāvī, cremātum (12)	1, to burn to ashes, cremate
crucem	see crux
crux, crucis (13)	f. cross
cum (6)	preposition + abl. - with
currō, currere, cucurrī, cursum (3)	3, to run
dē (1)	prep. + ablative, down from, concerning, about
decem (1)	indeclinable numerical adjective - ten
dēfessus, -a, -um (5)	adj. tired
dēleō, dēlēre, dēlēvī, dēlētum (10)	2, to destroy
dēmōnstrō, dēmōnstrāre, dēmōnstrāvī, dēmōnstrātum (7)	1, to point out, show
dēnique (5)	adv. finally
deus, -ī (6)	m. god
diēs, diēī (8)	m/f. day
Diocletianus, -ī (12)	m. Diocletian
domus, domūs (9)	m/f. house
dux, ducis (2)	m. leader
ē, ex (15)	prep. + ablative, out of, from
ecclēsia, ae (14)	f. church

edō, edere, ēdī, ēsum (6)	3, to eat
eheu (3)	interjection, alas!
elephantus, -ī (2)	m. elephant
eō, īre, iī, ītum (10)	irreg. verb, to go
ērumpō, ērumpere, ērūpī, ēruptum (11)	2, to burst out, erupt
et (2)	conj. and
exeō, exīre, exiī, exitum (15)	irreg. verb, to go out of/from
exerceō, exercēre, exercuī, exercitum (2)	2, to train
falsus, -a, -um (12)	adj. wrong, false
familia, -ae (15)	f. family
favus, -ī (6)	m. honeycomb
fēriae, -ārum (11)	f.pl. holidays, vacation
ferus, -a, -um (6)	adj. wild
fīlius, -ī (6)	m. son
flagrō, flagrāre, flagrāvī, flagrātum (9)	1, to burn to ashes, cremate
flamma, -ae (6)	f. flame, fire
Flavianus, -a, -um (9)	adj. Flavian, pertaining to the Flavian dynasty
forum, -ī (9)	n. market place, forum
gestō, gestāre, gestāvī, gestātum (6)	1, to wear
glōria, -ae (5)	f. glory
Graecus, -a, -um (1)	adj. Greek
habeō, habēre, habuī, habitum (2)	2, to have, hold
habitō, habitāre, habitāvī, habitātum (11)	1, to live, dwell
Hannibal, -is (2)	m. Hannibal
Herculāneum, -ī (11)	n. Herculaneum

Glossary

Herculus, -ī (12)	m. Hercules (demi-god and son of Juppiter)
Hierosolyma, -ōrum (10)	m.pl. Jerusalem
Iesus, -ī (5)	m. Jesus
imperātor, imperātōris (13)	m. emperor
imperium, -imperiī (4)	n. empire; command
in (4)	prep. + ablative, in, on; + accusative - into
ineō, inīre, iniī, initum (15)	irreg. verb, to go into, enter
inimīcus, -ī (3)	m., enemy (personal enemy)
Iohannes, Iohannis (6)	m. John
īrātus, -a, -um (3)	adj. angry
Ītalia, -ae (4)	f. Italy
iterum (13)	adv. - again
iubeō, iubēre, iussī, iussum (13)	2, to order
Iūdaeī, -ōrum (6)	m.pl. - Jews
Iūdaeus, -a, -um (8)	adj. Jewish
Iuppiter, Iovis (12)	m. Juppiter (Roman king of the gods)
iuxtā (9)	prep. + accusative, next to, near
Iosephus, -ī (5)	m. Joseph
liber, librī (1)	m. book
lōcusta, -ae (6)	f. locust
longus, -a, -um (10)	adj. long
maneō, manēre, mansī, manitum (4)	2, to remain, stay
Maria, ae (5)	f. Mary
Maximianus, -ī (12)	m. Maximian
memoria, -ae (15)	f. memory
mīrus, -a, -um (5)	adj. strange, wonderful

Glossary

moneō, monēre, monuī, monitum (6)	2, to warn
mōns, montis (11)	m. mountain
multus, -a, -um (1)	adj. many
mūrus, -ī (10)	m. wall
narrō, narrāre, narrāvī, narrātum (7)	1, to tell
necō, necāre, necāvī, necātum (1)	1, to kill, to execute
Nero, Nerōnis (9)	m. Nero
nihil (15)	adv. nothing, none, no more
nisi (12)	conj. unless
nōn (3)	adv. not
nūdus, -a, -um (9)	adj. bare, naked, nude
nunc (4)	adv. now
Octavius, -ī (4)	m. Octavian
odōrātus, -a, -um (5)	adj. smelly
omnipotens, omnipotentis (14)	adj. omnipotent, all powerful
oppidum, -ī (7)	n. town
oppugnō, oppugnāre, oppugnāvī, oppugnātum (2)	1, to attack
optō, optāre, optāvī, optātum (10)	1, to choose, want
parabola, -ae (7)	f. parable, proverb
parō, parāre, parāvī, parātum (6)	1, to prepare
pater, patris (14)	m. father
per (10)	prep. + accusative, through, during
plēnus, -a, -um (5)	adj. full
Pompēiī, -ōrum (11)	m.pl. Pompeii
pōnō, pōnere, posuī, positum (13)	3, to put, place
populus, -ī (3)	m. people

Glossary

portō, portāre, portāvī, portātum (5)	1, to carry
post (8)	adv. after; prep. + acc. - after
praemium, -ī (10)	n. reward, loot, prize
prehendō, prehendere, prehendī, prehensum (12)	3, to arrest
prōcēdo, prōcēdere, prōcessī, prōcessum (14)	3, to go forth, proceed
prohibeō, prohibēre, prohibuī, prohibitum (12)	2, to forbid
prope (9)	prep. + accusative, near
pugnō, pugnāre, pugnāvī, pugnātum (2)	1, to fight
Pūnicus, -a, -um (2)	adj. Carthaginian
quī (14)	pronoun, who
quod (8)	conj. because
regnum, -ī (7)	n. kingdom, rule, reign
regō, regere, rexī, rectum (4)	3, to rule
resurgō, resurgere, resurrexī, resurrectum	3, to rise again
rēx, rēgis (8)	m. king
Rōma, ae (15)	f. Rome
Rōmānī, -ōrum (2)	m, Romans
Rōmānus, -a, -um (1)	adj. Roman
ruīna, ae (9)	f. ruin, debris
sanctus, -a, -um (12)	adj. sacred, holy
scrībō, scrībere, scripsī, scriptum (1)	3, to write
scūtum, -ī (13)	n. shield
secundus, -a, -um (2)	adj. second
sed (5)	conj. but
sedeō, sedēre, sēdī, seditum (7)	2, to sit

Glossary

semper (8)	adv. always
senātor, senātōris (3)	m. senator
signum, -ī (8)	n. sign
simul (4)	adv. together, at the same time
sine (12)	prep. + ablative, without
sōlus, -a, -um (4)	adj. alone, only
sordidus, -a, -um (5)	adj. dirty
spīritus, spīritūs (14)	m. breath, spirit
stabulum, -ī (5)	n. stable
statua, -ae (9)	f. statue
subitō (11)	adv. suddenly
sum, esse, fuī, futūrum (1)	irreg. verb, to be
suprā (8)	prep. + accusative, above, over
templum, -ī (10)	n. temple
teneō, tenīre, tenuī, tentum (15)	2, to hold
timeō, timēre, timuī (8)	2, to fear, be afraid of
Titus, -ī (10)	m. Titus
tōtus, -a, -um (15)	adj. whole, all
trēs, tria (8)	numerical adj. three
unigenitus, -a, -um (14)	adj. only begotten
ūnus, -a, -um (14)	numerical adj. one
veniō, venīre, vēnī, ventum (5)	4, to come
Vesuvius, -ī (11)	m. Vesuvius
vexō, vexāre, vexāvī, vexātum (12)	1, to annoy, harass
victor, victōris (4)	m. victor, winner
videō, vidēre, vīdī, vīsum (8)	2, to see
vincō, vincere, vīcī, victum (13)	to win, conquer
vir, virī (2)	m. man

Glossary

Virtuvius Pollio (1)	m. Virtuvius Pollio, famous Roman architect
vīvificans, vīvificantis (14)	adj. lifegiver, giver of life
vīvus, -a, -um (8)	adj. alive, living

Latin For Children, Primer A
HISTORY READER

Bibliographia

Grammar References & Lexica

Allen and Greenough. <u>New Latin Grammar</u>. New Rochelle, NY: Caratza Aristiede D., 1992.

Crane, Gregory R. (ed.) <u>The Perseus Project, *http://www.perseus.tufts.edu, July 2004*</u>

Lewis and Short. <u>A Latin Dictionary</u>. Oxford: Clarendon Press, 1879.

Glare, et alii. <u>Oxford Latin Dictionary</u>. Oxford: Clarendon Press, 1982.

<u>The New College Latin & English Dictionary</u>, John C. Traupman,Ph.D., S Joseph's University, Philadelphia, 1966

Historical References

Cary, M. and H. H. Scullard. <u>A History of Rome</u>. St. Martin's Press, 1975

Detweiler, Marlin & Laurie. <u>New Testament, Greece & Rome History Series</u>. Pennsylvania: Veritas Press, 2001

Grant, Michael. <u>The Roman Emperors</u>. New York: Barnes & Noble Books, 1997.

Schaff, Philip (ed). <u>The Creeds of Christendom, Vol. I</u>. Baker Book Hous Company, 1990

Notes

Notes

Notes

Notes

About the Author

Karen Moore began her study of Latin in seventh grade, and added Greek to her linguistic studies during her college years. In 1994, she was awarded the Ruth and Myron G. Kuhlman Scholarship in Classics. Karen graduated from the University of Texas at Austin in 1996 with a Bachelor of Arts in Classics and a minor in History. Since that time she has taught Latin to students in grades three through twelve through a wide variety of venues, including homeschool, public school, and Classical Christian schools. She is currently serving as the chair of the Latin Department at Grace Academy of Georgetown, a Classical Christian school located in the heart of Texas. She is a member of the American Classical League, the Texas Classical Association, and serves as the sponsor of Grace Academy's Latin Club.

Karen and her husband, Bryan, have three children who attend school at Grace Academy.

About the Editor

Gaylan DuBose graduated with high honors from the University of North Texas in 1964 and received his Master of Arts in Classics from the University of Minnesota in 1970 He has also studied at the University of Texas and at Worcester College, Oxford University, England. He was the academic contest chair for the National Junior Classical League from 1996 through 2005. He currently is teaching at St. Andrew's Episcopal School in Austin, Texas, and is in his forty-third year as a classroom teacher. He is the author of Farrago Latina: A Teacher Resource and co-author of Excelability in Advanced Latin. He is an avid reader and is the organist and minister of music at St. Augustine's Orthodox Catholic Church and Pro-Cathedral in Pflugerville, Texas.

ANSWER KEY

Looking for the answers to this book?
Download and print the answers (PDF)
for <u>free</u> from our website at:

www.ClassicalAcademicPress.com

A fun free site to
practice your Latin!

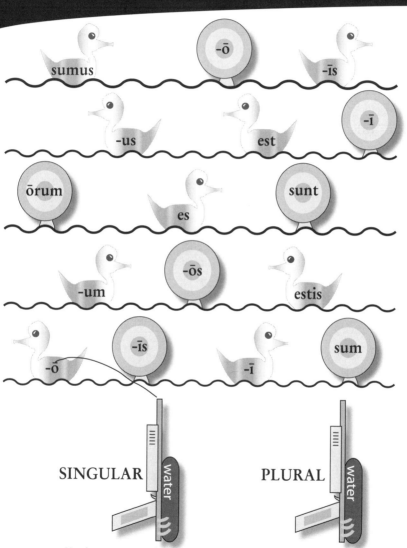

Use the water guns at the bottom to correctly connect (draw a line) to the 2nd Declension Noun ending. Can you do **Sum** (I am) as well?

CARNIVAL SHOOT OUT!

Are you looking for an understandable, engaging, and creative way to introduce your students to the ancient language of the New Testament? We are pleased to announce the coming release of *Greek for Children, Primer A*. *Greek for Children* has been designed to teach in the lively structure and method of the acclaimed *Latin for Children* Primer series. Like LFC, *Greek for Children* is designed to be used in grades three and up.

Why Greek? Koine Greek is a rich and fascinating language. Like Latin, it will aid students in critical thinking skills and a strong understanding of grammar. Many English words are derived from ancient Greek, and students will especially see the benefits of studying Greek when studying science and medicine. Last, but hardly least, Koine Greek is the language of the New Testament, and the study of the original language will gradually unveil the richness, depth and beauty of the New Testament message.

Greek for Children, Primer A is comprised of thirty two chapters, to be completed one per week. Each chapter will begin with a Memory Page, presenting the chant and vocabulary for the week's lesson. Grammar lessons will be presented at the student's level on the Grammar Page, and each chapter includes a worksheet and a quiz. An Answer Key and an audio files will also be available.

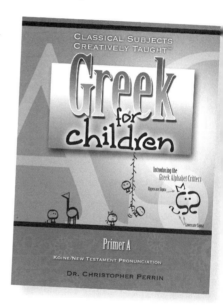

Samples online at: www.ClassicalAcademicPress.com